INTRODUCTION

Welcome to the first book in the series "A Heroes History". World War II was Britain's finest hour. The whole of society, men and women, old and young worked together to survive against great odds. Churchill's rousing speeches strengthened the morale in Britain, while Hitler began to lose his grip in Europe.

The home front, life as an evacuee and the role of women brought experiences which changed lives forever. Finally, the end of the war brought about by the explosion of the atomic bombs at Hiroshima and Nagasaki and the devastation unleashed by such catastrophic weapons, a lesson to mankind.

The discovery of death camps, where whole families had suffered and died in their millions was final proof of the inhumanity which man is capable of inflicting on his fellow man.

There have been many conflicts since 1945, but none have come close to the global impact of World War II.

CONTENTS

Written and Illustrated by Les Ives
Published by Colour History Ltd © 2004

Germany and Hitler

On the 11th of November 1918, World War I came to an end. In four dreadful years, over 12 million soldiers from across the globe had lost their lives in the bloodiest conflict the world had ever known.

The heaviest fighting occurred in the trenches and suffocating mud of France and Belgium. It was here that the armies of Germany battled against the forces of France, Great Britain and her Empire allies.

America entered the war in April 1917. The stalemate was finally broken and "the war to end all wars" had finally come to an end.

Economic Depression

Germany paid a heavy price for her defeat. At the Treaty of Versailles in 1919 she was forced to agree to pay huge financial compensation for war damage, as well as losing large frontier areas and worldwide colonies. Germany was allowed to keep a small army and navy. However, she was not aloud her air force or submarines.

Germany's economic recovery during the 1920's came to an abrupt halt in 1929 as America's economic boom came to an end. The Wall Street crash followed with the collapse of the New York stock Exchange and then the Great Depression.

America's problems soon enveloped the world. At the end of the First World war the USA had helped many European countries to re-build their shattered economies, with the Depression deepening, they now demanded re-payment.

Economic misery spread across Europe and in a weakened Germany the effect was devastating. Shares and savings became worthless, inflation rose and money had little value. By 1932 unemployment in Germany had reached six million and the nation was on its knees. The stage was now set for a new leader, his name - Adolf Hitler.

Once hitler was released from prison, the Nazi Party became increasingly popular. There were a number of reasons for this:

- Hitler's image was of a strong leader
- He shared the popular hatred of the Versailles Treaty
- He encouraged the belief that both communists and Jews were responsible for Germany's problems

The Nazi party became the largest party in the elections of 1932 and Hitler was appointed Chancellor in January 1933. In the following month the German Parliament building, the "Reichstag," was mysteriously burnt to the ground. A young communist was arrested and Hitler seized the opportunity to arrest many of his left wing political opponents. Upon the death of President Hindenburg in 1934, Hitler became President and gave himself a new title - Fuhrer, meaning leader. He was now in total control of his new nation - the Third Reich.

The Rise of Hitler

Adolf Hitler was born in Austria in 1889. An average school career was followed by his failure to be accepted as an art student, but his life in Vienna changed at the outbreak of WWI.

Hitler joined the German army in 1914 and proved to be a good soldier. At the end of the war, however, his hatred had grown for the people he saw as enemies of Germany. He found a passion for politics and he joined the right-wing National Socialist Party - the Nazis, and very quickly became their party leader.

Hitler formed the SA, a uniformed private army, who were soon brawling with their communist enemies in the streets of Germany. Encouraged by his new, if limited popularity, he planned to lead his SA stormtroopers from a Munich beer hall and overthrow the German government. The beer hall 'Putsch' was an embarrassing failure and Hitler was thrown into prison.

During his time in prison Hitler wrote his book 'Mein Kampf' ('My Struggle'). In it he outlined his plans for Germany and his views on racial purity.

How did the Depression help Hitler?

Why was the Nazi party more popular when Hitler was released from jail?

Road to War

Hitler's re-organisation of Germany was swift, ruthless and very effective. He identified key areas which would strengthen his power, including the labour force, state-control, youth and re-armament.

Labour

Germany's huge unemployment problem was tackled by introducing major construction schemes, such as motorways and new buildings. With the slogan 'Strength through Joy', workers were given benefits and cheap holidays. People were so grateful for work that Hitler was able to remove the right to go on strike.

State Control

On 30th June 1934 Hitler ordered 'The Night of the Long Knives,' sanctioning the murder of many of his old SA comrades. These unpopular men were replaced by Hitler's own personal bodyguard, the S.S. This organisation rapidly expanded, as did the feared secret police - the Gestapo. Personal freedom in Germany was effectively ended as anti-Nazi newspapers were shut down and listening to foreign radio stations was banned. Now all information came from the Ministry of Propaganda, run by Joseph Goebbels. Jewish synagogues were vandalised and Jewish shops and businesses were boycotted. Huge Nazi rallies were staged at Nuremberg to show the strength of the party and an increasing number of Jews, communists and other 'undesirables' were arrested. They were sent to prison without trial and eventually to concentration camps.

The Nazis staged huge rallies at Nuremberg.

Hitler youth members carried flags and played drums at Nazi rallies.

Youth

In school, pupils were taught of the greatness of Germany and the superiority of the blonde and fair skinned 'Ayrian' races of Northern Europe. Teachers who did not agree to the new curriculums were forced out of their jobs. From 1936 all young people were required to belong to the Hitler Youth movement, where camping and outdoor pursuits ran alongside the brainwashing of Nazi ideals into vulnerable young minds.

Re-armament

Within days of becoming leader, Hitler began to re-build Germany's armed forces. Secrecy surrounded his early plans. In 1935 Hitler openly defied the Treaty of Versailles by re-building the nation's military strength for the whole world to see. In 1936 all young German males were required to serve time in the forces. Military equipment was mass-produced from the country's re-vitalised factories, and with Hitler's confidence growing Germany was now ready to set-off on the long road to war.

Timeline of key dates:

- 1936 German troops re-enter the Rhineland, the neutral zone between Germany and France.

- 1937 Hitler lends military support to fascist leader General Franco, helping him to win the Spanish Civil War.

- 1938 German soldiers enter Austria to unify the two nations.

- 1938 Hitler announced his intention to occupy the German speaking Sudetenland, an area within Czechoslovakia. Britain and France, nervous of a new world war, met Hitler in Munich and agreed to his demands on the condition that there would be no further German military expansion. British Prime Minister, Neville Chamberlain, returned to a heroes welcome in the UK.

- 1939 Hitler ignored the Munich Agreement and invaded the rest of Czechoslovakia.

- 1939 Hitler and Stalin, the communist dictator of Russia, formed a Nazi-Soviet Pact. With temporary peace between the two nations, Hitler was able to concentrate on his European ambitions. Stalin strengthened his armies for a war that was now inevitable.

- 1939 Hitler maked unreasonable demands for land in Poland. His demands were ignored. On September 1st Hitler invaded Poland.

- 1939 With Britain and France's peace attempts lying in tatters, both countries were forced to declare war on Germany.

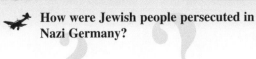

How were Jewish people persecuted in Nazi Germany?

Why did Hitler make young people join the Hitler youth movement?

Neville Chamberlain returns from Munich with the agreement he thought would mean "peace in our time."

Britain Goes to War

On 3rd September, 1939 Neville Chamberlain announced to the British nation that:

"This country is at war with Germany. May God bless us all. May he defend the right, for it is evil things that we shall be fighting against, brute force, bad faith, injustice, oppression and persecution; and against that I am certain that right will prevail."

While Britain prepared for war, Hitler's armies stormed through Poland. Using "Blitzkrieg," meaning lightning war, German fighter planes and dive bombers destroyed the polish air force while it was still on the ground. Roads and railways were destroyed and German panzers (tanks) and infantry cut through the brave, but old fashioned and badly equipped Polish armies. Within a month Hitler had control of western Poland and Stalin was given control of the east.

Preparing for War

A period of nervous calm now descended on Europe. Along the border with Germany, the French manned their heavily defended forts, known as the "Maginot line." In the meantime the British army moved to the Belgian border.

Back in Britain an Act was passed, requiring all men between the ages of eighteen and forty-one to be called upon for service in the forces. Sign posts were removed throughout the country in case of an invasion and gas masks were issued to protect people from gas attack. Food rationing was also introduced.

Throughout the winter of 1939/40 there was very little activity, but in April Germany launched a lightning attack on Denmark and Norway. Allied assistance came too late and Denmark was forced to surrender. Norway held out bravely for a few months. Public anger in Britain forced the resignation of Neville Chamberlain. On the 10th of May, 1940 Winston Churchill became the new Prime Minister of Great Britain.

On the day that Churchill became Prime Minister, Hitler ordered his troops to attack France.

Invasion of France

Using the same 'blitzkrieg' tactics, Germany's mechanised forces stormed through the weakly defended countries of Holland and Belgium. France's 'Maginot Line' was effectively ignored, as the Germans swept around it and advanced rapidly through the low countries.

Such was the speed of their advance that the allied armies were now effectively cut in half. The British army in the north and the French in the south. In danger of being overwhelmed, the British army retreated to the costal town of Dunkirk. It was here that 340,000 allied soldiers were rescued by the royal navy and an armada of commercial and private boats. A huge amount of equipment was lost, but vital manpower was saved.

200,000 British and 140,000 French soldiers were evacuated from the beaches of Dunkirk.

The German advance was unstoppable. With their superior tactics and equipment the French were easily overpowered. Paris fell on 14th June and eight days later a peace treaty was signed between the two nations.

Hitler now had total control of northern France while Marshall Petain, a French First World War General was allowed to run a German controlled government in the south.

With almost total control of northern Europe, on the 14th of July 1940, Hitler announced a new plan, Operation 'Seelöwe'(Sealion), the proposed invasion of Great Britain.

What happened the day Churchill became Prime Minister?

What was operation 'Sea Lion'?

German troops parade down the Champs-Elysees, Paris in June 1940.

The Battle of Britain

Hitler's plan for the invasion of Britain involved a huge seaborne invasion. Without control of the air, however Operation 'Sea Lion' had very little chance of success.

Under the command of Reichmarshal Hermann Goring, the German "Luftwaffe" (air force), was an experienced and confident fighting force. They had been used in both the Spanish Civil War and the Blitzkrieg campaigns of Northern Europe, Goring had approximately 2500 aircraft at his disposal.

Spearheaded by fighter aircraft like the Messerschmitt 110 and 109's, the Luftwaffe also used the Junker 87 (Stuka) dive bomber, the Heinkel 111 and Dornier 17 bombers.

Facing the Luftwaffe were the Royal Air Force who were unable to call upon more than 1000 planes. They lacked pilots and battle experience. Alongside British airmen were pilots from New Zealand, Canada, Australia, South Africa and a small number from the still neutral America. Additional pilots who had escaped the German advances in Europe, from countries such as Poland, Czechoslovakia and France, helped to swell the RAF's ranks. Often with as little as ten hours flying experience, the pilots of the RAF faced massive odds. However, other factors helped them to make an impact:

• The excellence of the allied fighter planes including the fast and deadly Spitfires and the tough, manoeuvrable Hurricanes.

• The Germans had to fly long distances, leaving their fighter planes only limited time over Britain.

• A chain of 50 radar stations along the coast of England enabled the early detection of German airborne attacks.

• The increasingly patriotic nature of Churchill's speeches rallied the nation and prepared everyone for the fight, which lay ahead.

Excerpt from a speech made by Churchill at the beginning of the Battle of Britain.
"Let us therefore brace ourselves to our duties, so that if the British Empire lasts for a thousand years, men will say: "This was their finest hour".

Hawker Hurricane - This plane was not as fast, or able to fly as high as the German Messerschmitt. The Hurricane was, nevertheless, a manoeuvrable and well built plane. It was the most commonly used British fighter throughout the Battle of Britain.

Messerschmitt Me 109E – This German fighter plane was capable of speeds exceeding 350 mph, only the Spitfire was faster. A single seater aircraft it was armed with machine guns and shell firing cannons. It proved a formidable opponent for the planes of the RAF.

The Battle of Britain began in early July 1940 with bombing of shipping along England's south coast. Over the next few weeks German bombers, with fighter support, began raiding RAF bases and radar installations.

During the summer months the battle raged over the skies of Surrey and Kent. Casualties rose on both sides. The lack of trained manpower and planes was of great concern to Air Chief Marshall Dowding, the chief of RAF fighter command. The scarcity of planes and pilots made it essential to keep a reserve force safely on the ground in readiness for new attacks. The British were forced to send much smaller formations to attack the large waves of German fighters and bombers.

The attacking German planes were picked up by coastal radar. Once over Britain however the formations would break-up and attack various targets. Increasingly it became difficult for the thinly spread British fighters to cover all of the possible target areas.

Hitler's patience was running. In September Goring was ordered to concentrate his squadrons on a new campaign, attacking civilian targets in Great Britain. This was designed to damage the population's morale.

By early October the Battle of Britain was effectively won, for the people of Britain's major cities it had only just begun.

Excerpt from a speech made by churhill at the height of the battle, August 1940.
"never in the field of human conflict was so much owed by so many to so few"

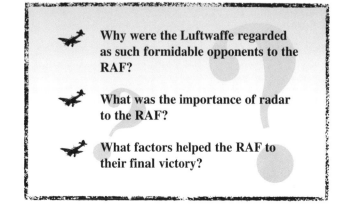

Spitfires shoot down a Junker Ju 88 bomber.

The Luftwaffe extended their bombing raids and attacked the naval dockyards at Portsmouth and the maritime towns of Bristol and Liverpool. These raids caused great damage and loss of service and civilian life.

To the increasing frustration of Goring the Luftwaffe's numerical superiority could not swing the battle his way. The RAF squadrons were organised, determined and in a constant state of alert. Exhausted pilots were often "scrambled," inflicting serious losses on the German formations. The Luftwaffe's early battle confidence began to drain away, as their casualties mounted.

Why were the Luftwaffe regarded as such formidable opponents to the RAF?

What was the importance of radar to the RAF?

What factors helped the RAF to their final victory?

The Blitz

In the autumn of 1940 Hitler tried a new strategy in his efforts to defeat Great Britain. Using large bomber formations to attack major towns and cities, he set out to undermine the morale of the British civilian population and destroy the country's industry and communications.

The Blitz began on 7th September 1940. Bombs rained down on the docklands and streets of London's East End. When the raid finally ended in the early hours of the following morning, over four hundred people had lost their lives in the smoking ruins.

There was now little respite for the people of London. From the 7th of September through to the 13th November, England's capital was bombed on sixty-seven out of sixty-eight consecutive nights. Waves of up to 700 Luftwaffe bombers released an avalanche of incendiary (firebomb) and explosive bombs and the hard pressed London fire service battled to save a city in flames.

Finding Shelter

Thousands of people poured into the London Underground stations for safety. Others found refuge in purpose-built bomb shelters, cellars, basements and even Church crypts. Some families built their own concrete shelters, while the Government issued over a million Anderson shelters to poorer families. These consisted of sheets of bolted steel, which were sunk into the ground and then covered with earth. They were often cold, damp and without toilets, but they saved many lives.

Air Raid Wardens (ARP's) patrolled the streets and shelters with squads of volunteers, they worked tirelessly to rescue survivors and helped to repair gas, water and electricity supplies.

The RAF and anti-aircraft batteries attacked the German bomber formations whenever they could. Massive barrage balloons were floated in the sky to obstruct their path, but the raids continued.

To help hide the city in darkness a blackout was introduced. Homes used extra thick curtains, street lighting was switched off and all vehicle headlights were reduced to the barest minimum of light.

In November 1940 Hitler ordered more bombing raids over Britain. Waves of Heinkel bombers attacked many of the nation's major towns. On November 14th over 500 tonnes of bombs were dropped on Coventry, the centre of Britain's ammunition manufacturing. Massive destruction was caused in the city and its industrial areas. However, within five days most of the 21 key amunition factories were back in full production. People returned to work to help clear-up the rubble and replace damaged roofs with tarpaulin sheets. Heating for the shattered factories was provided by temporary coal fires. The determination to carry on working was repeated throughout the country.

The Luftwaffe bombing raids extended from the south coast of England to Clydebank in Scotland and included both industrial and historical towns.

In an effort to cut off vital food and other supplies from abroad, major coastal ports such as Glasgow, Liverpool, Hull and Swansea were attacked with devastating results. Even historical towns such as Exeter, Canterbury and York were not spared.

The Blitz lasted until May 1941 as Hitler now turned his attentions to the German invasion of Russia. Raids on mainland Britain were now rapidly scaled down. Of the 60,000 civilian casualties in the country during World War II, 40,000 perished during the Blitz. Over 54,000 tonnes of bombs were dropped and around 2,000,000 homes were destroyed, along with factories and docklands.

However, the raids did have some positive benefits to contribute towards Britain's morale, as Germany failed to weaken British resolve. There was a feeling of shared hardship, which brought people from different backgrounds together. The country was united with one common goal - the defeat of Hitler.

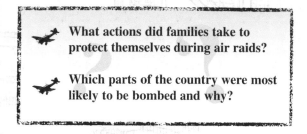

What actions did families take to protect themselves during air raids?

Which parts of the country were most likely to be bombed and why?

12

Evacuation

From the outbreak of war in 1939, the British Government feared the mass bombing of its towns and cities. One of the first major decisions of the war was to organise the evacuation of children from areas most at risk from bombing and move them to the safety of the countryside.

The first batches of children were evacuated in "Operation Pied Piper" on 1st September, 1939. After the "phoney war" in the winter of 1939/40, many felt it was safe to return, with the onset of the blitz in November 1940, however the evacuation of thousands of children began.

Unaware of their final destination, children were taken to the large city railway stations. They travelled with only a small suitcase or bag, containing clothes, food for one day, a box containing a gas mask and a label bearing their name, school and station of departure. A few mothers accompanied very young children. For many it was the first time they had been separated from their parents. It was a bewildering and frightening experience.

Towns and villages were checked to find out how many evacuees they were able to take. Children arrived at local train stations to be picked up by the people accommodating them. Known as billets, it was compulsory for families to take in children. A payment was received for the number of evacuees they looked after.

By Christmas of 1940 more than 1.5 million children, pregnant women and other vulnerable people, such as the disabled, had been evacuated to safer areas of the country.

Children could take only a few possessions and their final destination was unknown to them.

Life as an Evacuee

Evacuees were generally aged between five and fourteen. A large number of the children came from the tightly packed, smoggy streets of Britain's major cities. With limited bathing facilities and poor health care, many evacuees had infections such as ringworm and impetigo. Headlice were also very common and country pet stores ran out of animal de-lousing combs very quickly!

Often evacuated to rural areas, the children were able to help on farms, caring for the animals and enjoying fresh air and better diets. The lifestyle and general health of many city children improved during their years as evacuees.

Not all children enjoyed their experiences. Children from wealthier families could find themselves billeted in homes without an indoor toilet and a tin bath to bathe in.

Some children were very homesick and tried to return to their own homes in the cities. Special shows and concerts were organised by local communities to entertain the children and help them feel more settled. The WVS (Women's Voluntary Service) did a great deal to help children cope with their time away from home.

A large number of teachers were evacuated with their pupils. Many retired teachers came back into schools to help with the increasing numbers of evacuees arriving in rural areas. Often short of space, some lessons were taught in local churches and village halls.

Evacuees were billeted with families until the end of the war. Moving large numbers of children to areas they did not know, often to staying with families from very different backgrounds, was an experience that most children would never forget.

A gas mask in a cardboard box and an identity label was issued to all evacuees.

What were the main reasons for evacuating children to the countryside?

Imagine you were billeted in the country, away from your home. Write a letter to your parents in the city where you lived, telling them how you are and how your life has changed.

Life in Britain

Cut off from mainland Europe, Britain was isolated in the early years of the war. Dependant on the world for much of its food and raw materials, the government had to act quickly to introduce measures to ensure the countrys survival.

Food

Every family was issued with a ration book. Each person was entitled to a ration of essential food per week and provisions were only given on the production of ration book coupons. Many imported goods, such as coffee and fruit, vanished from the shelves and creative methods of cooking soon appeared. Dried acorns were used instead of coffee and hot beetroot in white sauce often replaced meat. Powdered egg was a cheap substitute to supplement fresh rationed eggs. If "luxury" products did arrive in the shops, long queues formed outside.

The weekly food ration for one person
One egg
2 oz Cooking fat
8 oz Sugar
4 oz Bacon or ham
2 oz Margarine
2 oz Tea
10 oz Cheese
Meat to the value of 1 shilling 2d

Re-cycling

The Government encouraged the re-cycling of materials to help the war effort. Thousands of school children saved aluminium from bottle tops. Tin was removed from baths and iron was re-cycled from railways, bicycles, gates and bedsteads.

Clothes

Sixty-six coupons a year were issued to buy clothing. The coupons were exchanged, together with cash to purchase new clothes and shoes. People were encouraged to keep their clothes longer and to make their own wherever possible. Fashions changed and clothing was manufactured using less cloth. Suit jackets became single breasted, skirts became shorter and trousers were produced without turn ups, or pockets. Make-up became scarce and brown boot polish was often used to colour women's legs, as silk stockings were in very short supply.

Land

The "Dig for Victory" campaign was a Government idea to persuade farmers and ordinary people to make more land available to grow extra food. Lawns, railway embankments and even public parks were turned into allotments.

The U-Boat Menace

Hitler was well aware of Britain's dependence on supplies from abroad. Under the command of Admiral Dönitz, Germany's fleet of U-boat submarines were instructed to sink allied shipping and close Britain's vital supply lines from America.

Large and slow moving Atlantic convoys were easy prey for the fast and virtually undetectable U-boat packs. In the first year of the war 114 allied ships were sunk and by 1942, six million tonnes of shipping had been destroyed, with the loss of over 30,000 merchant seamen.

U-boats set off from the captured naval bases of Norway and France and with only a relatively short distance to travel they were able to attack the convoys on a regular basis.

When Hitler attacked Russia in June 1941, Stalin was desperate for more arms and ammunition. To help his Russian allies, Churchill ordered merchant convoys to sail the dangerous Baltic route to Russia. Sailing close to German controlled Norway, the allied ships were attacked from both sea and air. When the battered convoys reached the Russian ports they had often lost half of their numbers.

Britain responded by increasing her air support and better equipping the escort ships, especially their radar. When America entered the war in December 1941, more commercial shipping became available and long range American bombers were able to track and attack U-boats, which previously had been out of range.

The U-boat menace remained until the end of the war. The early days of the 1940's were the most perilous to the survival of Britain's vital Atlantic lifeline.

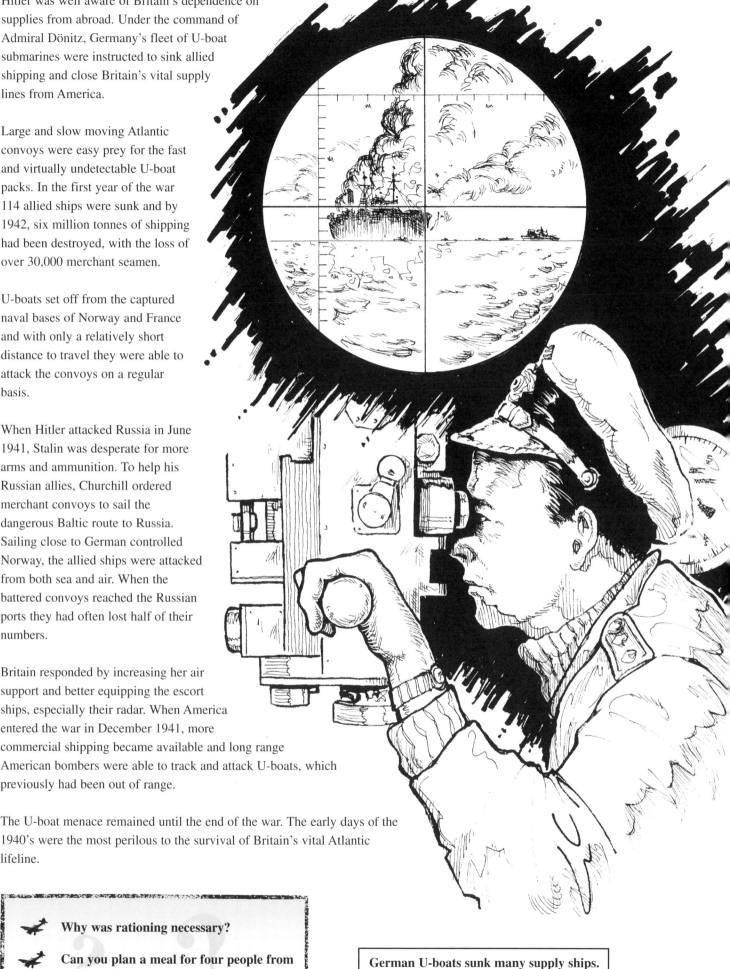

German U-boats sunk many supply ships.

 Why was rationing necessary?

 Can you plan a meal for four people from the list of food rations on the opposite page?

Britain's War Effort

The role of women before war broke out in 1939 was largely dedicated to raising children and looking after the home. As their men folk went off to war their situation dramatically changed.

The nation was faced with huge shortfalls in its public and industrial workforce. The government began to encourage women to fill these positions in order to maintain vital services.

Industry

British industry had to gear itself to the war effort. As the men joined the forces, female workers were rapidly introduced onto the production lines. After some initial resistance to them, female employees soon began to prove their worth and quickly became essential workers in the ammunition and tank factories, while seamstresses produced everything from uniforms to parachutes.

Public Services

Women were quick to take on public service duties too, such as clerical work, driving, and conducting road and rail services. Many more became ambulance drivers and fire brigade officers, rescuing people and fighting fires in Britain's blitzed cities. The WVS (Women's Voluntary Service) grew to over a million strong, running canteens, nurseries for working mothers and helping to settle evacuated children.

Land Girls

77,000 young women joined the Women's Land Army working on farms across the country, facing some initial hostility. However, through hard work and determination they soon proved themselves, helping to harvest, plough and bring in the crops essential to the nation's survival.

Women's Services

Although women were not allowed to fight, they were encouraged to join the armed forces in supporting roles.

ATS

Auxiliary Territorial Service. This was the female wing of the regular Army. Women became nurses, lorry drivers, sentries, manned search lights and undertook plane spotting duties. At their peak in1944, the ATS had nearly 200,000 members.

WAAF

Women's Royal Auxiliary Air Force. Women played a vital role in the RAF control centres. They worked in teams, tracking the path of enemy squadrons attacking the country.

WRENS

The Women's Royal Navy Service. Working as river pilots, radio operators and maintaining ships in dry dock.

Red Cross

Thousands of women were employed as nurses and medics in hospitals throughout Britain and abroad.

SOE

A small group of very brave young women worked with the Special Operatins Executive. Together with their male colleagues they were parachutted into German occupied Europe. Working closely with local resistance fighters they took part in dangerous syping operations and helped to destroy German railways and communication systems.

Living in constant danger many of them were arrested by the German secret police, the Gestapo. They were often tortured and finally executed.

Home Guard

In order to use as much of the nation's manpower as possible, the Government asked for older men to train in a new organisation, the Local Defence Volunteers (LDV). The LDV trained in their own clothes using old, or even wooden rifles to practice their drills!

As the war progressed the LDV became known affectionately as the "Home Guard". By 1943 there were two million members, now with proper uniforms and real weapons. They manned anti-aircraft guns, search light batteries and trained in the dangerous work of bomb disposal.

The war effort called upon people of both sexes and all ages, the vast majority responding in large numbers and with great enthusiasm.

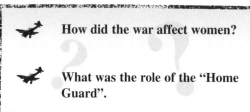

How did the war affect women?

What was the role of the "Home Guard".

Road to Victory

By 1943 the tide of the war was turning in favour of the allies. Victories in Africa and Hitler's crushing defeat at Stalingrad had destroyed the invincible image of the German armies.

Europe

On 6th June, 1944 the allied supreme commander General Eisenhower ordered the beginning of 'Operation Overlord'. Known as D-Day, thousands of American, British and Canadian troops were landed on the beaches of Normandy in France. After a period of fierce fighting a beach head was established and the liberation of Europe had begun.

Months of heavy fighting followed, as the allies fought their way across France. On 25th August, 1944 Paris was liberated. Italy was invaded in the south and the Russian armies continued their huge offensive against the battered German armies in the east.

In February 1945 allied forces crossed the river Rhine into Germany. By the end of the month, Russian soldiers were only 60 km from Berlin. The city was soon under siege and on 30th April 1945, Adolf Hitler committed suicide in his underground bunker. On 7th May 1945, Germany surrendered and the war in Europe was over.

The atomic bomb attacks on Japan bring an end to World War II

Pacific

Germany's main wartime allies were Italy in the west and Japan in the east. After their surprise attack on the American fleet at pearl harbour, Japan had made spectacular land gains in the Pacific and Indian oceans. Burma, Malaysia, Singapore and the Philippines fell swiftly and Japan began to threaten south towards Australia and east towards the U.S.A.

The war began to turn in the allies favour when the Americans won the huge naval battles of Coral Sea and Midway in 1943. Slowly, but surely, allied armies fought their way around the Pacific. Horrific battles took place, as individual islands were re-captured from the fanatical Japanese. From the skies Kamikaze (suicide) pilots flew their planes into allied ships, willingly sacrificing their own lives to sink enemy shipping.

With virtually all of her empire lost and under constant bombing, Japan still refused all requests to surrender. Fearing a final bloodbath on Japanese soil, the allies took the decision to use the newly invented atomic bomb. On the 6th and 9th August, 1945 the Japanese cities of Hiroshima and Nagasaki were completely destroyed, with a huge loss of life. Five days later World War II was finally over.

V.E. Day

Victory in Europe (V.E. Day) was met with scenes of great celebration in Britain. Winston Churchill waved to huge crowds in London and the whole country celebrated with a sea of union jacks. Street parties and bonfires went on long into the night, as nearly six years of hardship and conflict came to an end.

As servicemen were demobilised from the forces, they handed back their uniforms in exchange for a new suit. Along with thousands of evacuated children they were able to return home. With many towns in ruins, housing was in short supply and more than 150,000 pre-fabricated homes were erected to house the many homeless families. Life was slow to return to normal. Rationing of food and clothes continued, as Britain and other nations began to re-build their cities, farms and factories.

Many soldiers returned to pre-fabricated homes.

The Cost

As the leaders of Nazi Germany were put on trial in Nuremburg for their war crimes, the world was able to count the cost of this terrible war.

An estimated 55 million people, soldiers and civilians, had lost their lives in this worldwide conflict. The horror and suffering was widespread, but the discovery of the Nazi concentration camps was the most shocking. Hitler's attempt to exterminate the European Jewish population had resulted in Jews and others being herded into camps, where they were gassed, beaten, or simply starved to death. An estimated 6,000,000 Jews perished in death camps such as Auschwitz and Belsen.

Cities across the globe had been left in ruins. Industries were destroyed and whole populations displaced. For world leaders the task of re-building was enormous.

Many wars have been fought since 1945, but none have come close to the global scale of World War II .

The Nazis called their persecution of the Jews the "final solution." It was their attempt to wipe out the Jewish race in Europe.

 What was "Operation Overlord"?

 Why was the atomic bomb used against Japan?

 Imagine you were a child on VE day in Britain. Write a diary note explaining what you did on V.E. Day and your hopes for the future.

**Battle of Britain
July-October 1940**

**Attack on Pearl Harbour
December 7th 1941**

**Allied victory at El Alamein
October 1942**

**German surrender at Stalingrad
January 21st 1943**

**D-Day landings in France
June 6th 1944**

**Atomic bomb dropped on
Hiroshima August 6th 1945**

World War II Date File

1939

September 1st	Hitler invades Poland
September 3rd	Britain and France declare war on Germany

1940

April 9th	Hitler invades Denmark and Norway
May 10th	Hitler invades Belgium and the Netherlands
May 27-June 4th	Evacuation of British and French troops from Dunkirk
June 14th	German troops enter Paris
June 22nd	France signs peace treaty with Germany
July-October	Battle of Britain
September-Oct	London and Coventry are blitzed

1941

May-June	Hitler invades Greece, Crete and Yugoslavia
May 27th	The Royal Navy sink the pride of the German fleet, the 'Bismark'
June 22nd	"Operation Barbarossa"- Hitler's invasion of Russia
December 7th	Japanese attack on the American naval base at Pearl Harbour

1942

February 15th	The British surrender Singapore to the Japanese
May 8th	American victory at Battle of Coral Sea against the Japanese
June 4th	American victory at Midway against the Japanese
August	The Battle of Stalingrad begins between Russia and Germany
October-Nov	Allied victory at Battle of El Alamein in Africa

1943

January 21st	German surrender at Stalingrad
May 13th	German and Italian surrender in Africa
July-August	Allied invasion of Sicily and Italy

1944

June 6th	D-Day - allied troops make landings in Normandy, France
August 25th	Allied troops liberate Paris
December 16th	'Battle of the Bulge' major German offensive in the Ardennes

1945

January 17th	Russian troops enter Warsaw in Poland
March-April	American assaults on Pacific Islands Iwo Jima and Okinawa
April 30th	Hitler commits suicide
May 2nd	German surrender in Italy
May 7th	Germany surrenders to the American Supreme Commander, General Eisenhower. V.E. Day
August 6th	Atomic bomb dropped on Hiroshima
August 9th	Atomic bomb dropped on Nagasaki
August 14th	Japan surrenders. War ends - V.J. Day (Victory over Japan)